The Roads Don't Love You

Kendall A. Bell

Maverick Duck Press
© 2018
www.maverickduckpress.com

- for Danielle

Praise for *The Roads Don't Love You*

Kendall Bell's new poetry book takes its readers down a road lined with secrets, shames, and the small triumphs of the every day. Each poem is a gorgeous portrait of reality presented dark-side-up, presented by voices that revel in the brutality of being slowly and irreversibly worn down by the grind. This collection will shatter you in the best possible way.

– Holly Day, poet, writer.

The Roads Don't Love You is an epoxy of emotion, concrete imagery, and metaphor. The poems and the reader's mind become bonded in a way as haunting as the poems themselves. Separation is a difficult experience.

- Don Kloss, author of *Big Time* and *Gnawing On A Friend*

Kendall A. Bell writes the kind of poetry I want to read. He should have gotten a book deal by now. His poems have no tidy endings just like real life. The poems play chicken; do not swerve from telling the darker side of modernity and relationships. His voice seeks to express humanity in a world of uncertainty and shopping malls - the new tombstones to god.

- Kate O'Shea, author of *Crackpoet*

In *The Roads Don't Love You*, Kendall A. Bell stays true to his voice, and the honesty and openness he has written with in the many chapbooks he has released over much time. It is a bare and vulnerable voice that is both uncompromising and free of pretense. In these poems is humanity, compassion and the need for deep connection.

-Taylor Emily Copeland, author of *Monarch* and *Caffeine kisses and long sleeves*

A landslide's brought me to a straight road empty...

You are the fire in my spine. Leave no shadow, take away my sorrow…

Tear in my side, I feel it all...

Meet me at the back of the crowd, this could be our time to slip away...

They try to fix you but sorrow's in the marrow...

Hiding out in trenches I've built, I'm so good at it now, I know how to trick myself...

A landslide's brought me to a straight road empty...

Watching Alicia

About ten minutes afterwards,
turned towards each other
I watched Alicia sleep.
Any thoughts of guilt evaporated.
The act of fucking
was too dirty to apply to what we did.

Not like when I took my then 17 year old girlfriend
to one of those pay-by-the-hour motels
out of embarrassment and fear
of being walked in on by someone in the house.

With Alicia, it might not have been love,
but there was enough.

We spoke of the things that excited us
and made the blood rush through our bodies
at a frenzied pace.
Things like music and poetry,
movies and favorite foods.
Things that I hadn't talked about
with that kind of passion in a long time.

To see her physically respond during a conversation
excited me as much as seeing her
in very short shorts.
Her tan seemed to make her hair look darker,
as it swirled around the white pillow cover,
like black ringlets spilled on a canvas.
A perfect frame frozen on a television screen.

She stirred for a moment and then inched towards me,
wrapped her honeyed arms around my pale body,
intertwined her smooth legs around mine.
You make me think I can be happy, she said.

Our Mutual Acquaintances
For Todd

Are in institutions and jails.
Some have decided to give up
by driving in front of trains.

There was the son of a psychiatrist,
your ex-girlfriend's brother,
who lost his mind
and knifed his parents to death.

The crazy eyed guy
you worked with at Herman's
who had a penchant for shiny shirts.
He mowed down a bunch of people
in New York City one afternoon.

Girls and boys
we walked high school hallways with
felled by cancer,
car accidents and drowning.

We don't give a second thought
about waking the next morning.

Made To Heal

The slice of flesh, red, and then
pinked just days ago, is not a
tiny sliver of black scab. You
follow the rise and fall, the
crash and burn, wash down the day
with whatever keeps you numb. It
is sunset and sundown, the bone
that strengthens after the break.
Her scent no longer lingers in the
dark hallway. There are no more
early morning floor creaks. You
lock the door, drive away from the
night terrors and into the cliche
of a rising sun, the wheels, the
air, the metal, carrying something
borne of hope.

Scintillation

The stars swallow us whole,
keep our outlines traced
in its ravenous belly.
Allowing us to contort,
to mold into each other
poses of comfort, of passion
while the scenery passes by -
a speedboat, cars rushing.
They are spectators, witnesses.
In between the touching,
the lips pressed
the bent bodies
our secret is kept.
We mark the earth below us
drag our feet in side by side x's
swear to meet in the same spot
under the same stars.
It is never enough.

Aftermath

These thick trunks
shudder with dents
and deep gashes
the rings ache

After a battering of wind
the branches droop
now they hang languid
in the still air

The leaves are two
three colors
blending with the ground
spilled around the knotted roots
this is what the seasons leave behind

Yet
it only hurts when I breathe

Freefall

Her voice, a safe haven from the
rituals that push him to the bottom
of bottles of the deepest red wine and
the edges of black, steel balconies.

Her outstretched arms measure the distance
between love and lust,
give him warmth instead of fire.

He carries things away from the scene:
the shape of her mouth on
the crumpled up napkin in his pocket,
the taste of strawberry on his lips,
the blood rush,
the fear of knowing that
skin trade is always dangerous play.

They trade secrets through open air,
steal minutes from the ticking clock,
make denial an art form,
while the branches snap around them
and send them spiraling into freefall.

Shotgun
For Liam

A shotgun blast ended it.
It was certainly the poetic way out.
Something must have weighed heavier
than the cancer
and a faulty heart.

A shotgun blast ended it.
There was the obligatory note
found by his wife,
now a weeping,
leafless Tree.

A shotgun blast ended it.
His name added to a dubious list.
Sexton, Plath, Berryman, Teasdale -
now Rector.

A shotgun blast.
A mess for someone to clean up.
A puddle of what gathered inside spilled,
for others to navigate through.

I was never familiar with his work,
only the despair.

Dancer
for Selma Jezkova

You accepted the noose.
Its threads
bristling against your neck.
The hood was too much.
You needed to breathe.

The sacrifice was fine with you.
You would be able to spare your son
your fate.

Your sight, stolen,
like the money you squirreled away,
by someone you trusted.
Like your dreams of dancing.

Your movements are fluid in your head.

You left singing.
The bottom dropped out quickly
and you undoubtedly felt little.

The truth of your hardships,
buried with you.

Rebirth

When you walk into the kitchen that isn't yours,
you find her wearing your shirt and nothing else
holding a large mug of coffee,
which she hands to you as she leans in
and kisses you hard.
The mug is hot, so you rest it
on the cold granite counter
where it makes a clunking noise.
Your hands slip around her waist.
So few mornings have started this way
in so many years that you've nearly forgotten
the taste of lust at sunrise.
The feel of her pale leg moving against yours
makes you forget about the years spent
trying to make a passionless marriage work.
There is now: you and her draped on each other
her long, brown hair enveloping your pale shoulder.

You are the fire in my spine. Leave no shadow, take away my sorrow...

Why I wasn't there for your mother's wake

I would not see your mother unwrapping
a root beer barrel and placing it
in her mouth slowly.
She would not be cutting off an oversized
piece of chocolate bundt cake for me,
or offering me the same kinds of food
I'd constantly reject, like potato salad.
It wouldn't be you and I hanging around in
your small bedroom playing Strat-o-matic baseball
rolling dice and reading results off of cards
while she would yell "Todd?!" up the stairs
after the phone rang.
I would be in a room full of somber people
telling you "I'm sorry.", while your long face
stretched longer, grew almost more Nordic,
like hers.
People shaking hands with you, trading awkward hugs.
And me, thinking about the stillness of the body,
the moment when your wife sent me the message
telling me she died that night.

Omens

Other kids told us that if we wanted
the swing to go higher, we needed to
tuck our legs back, then push them
back out while we swing. It was the
only way to get the kind of height
we wanted. Rich would furiously pump
his legs, pushing himself nearly
parallel with the top bar, the entire
structure shaking. I would slow down,
drag my heels along the dirt below
and rest, but he would leap from the
seat and hurl himself into the night
air, come crashing down into dandelion
dotted grass. He never broke a bone,
rolled over on his back and laughed
hysterically. I have been dragging
my feet every day since then.

Winterlong

I wait winterlong for you to wake
from a slumber that has kept your
long limbs immobile.

Your night stand has become a
mausoleum, nothing disturbed
from when you last touched it:
your alarm clock frozen at 11:14,
your hair brush, half off the stained wood
with long, blonde pieces of you in it.

Every night I visit the sterile space
you encompass now, watch your fingers
and toes in hopes that they respond when
I sing your favorite song, fill the room
with tulips of every color.

When spring arrives, your garden blooms
and I swear I see you carrying a watercan,
hear the buzz of your name on the honeybees,
hold the hope that you will bloom again
among the machines that hold your breath.

Cross country

The wailing begins again at 3am,
so he wills his sleep-heavy body
out from under blanket warmth,
his wife's curled body motionless
as he rises from the bed.
Heavy feet arrive at the infant's
room. He raises her to his shoulder
and sways back and forth to
the mating of crickets and house
sounds while he walks towards the
coat closet, finds his spring jacket.
The episode is over quickly,
her late-night terrors subsided.
He gently tucks her back under her
pink blanket and creeps out.
Digs into deep pockets searching for
a lighter, sneaks into the backyard to smoke,
into the garage to contemplate, into the car,
out onto a long stretch of highway to find
the life he imagined twenty years ago,
far away from suburbia.

The Falling

First, it was the mall
on an early Saturday evening,
my arms draped like butcher slabs
over the cool, silver railing,
then a slip, hands slide off the rail,
head first, turning -
air rushing around me and then -
my head rises, a gasp,
a bead of sweat.
The first of many tumbles.

The Empire State Building,
the Grand Canyon,
The Golden Gate Bridge.

Everywhere I've been, I've fallen.
My body a sacrifice to my brain,
a dead man walking.

The plan is simple:
avoid escalators,
stay five feet away from railings,
release my grip from anything,
anyone,
that pulls me to the edge.

She lost a hand to carpal tunnel

And I'm supposed to teach her how to read
while she teaches herself how to
write with her right hand.

This woman who does volunteer work and
whose only son kidnapped when he was five.

I listen to her speak words in a children's reader
and get distracted by how the stump on
her left arm holds the book down,
how she stumbles over words I take for granted,
like Wednesday,
and almost feel ashamed of myself
for complaining about my aching shoulder
and a nagging cough.

When she doesn't show up for class
on both Monday and Tuesday,
I start to wonder what else
has been taken from her
or if she's decided to give up entirely.

Trying to think of what I'd say to Brittany

I would tell her that I couldn't possibly know
why a fourteen year old girl would hang herself.
I would tell her that this life isn't always
worth fighting for, but at fourteen
nothing could ever be that terrible,
that heartbreaking, that painful for you to
take that rope and slip it
around the tender flesh of your neck.

Brittany, people will always break your heart,
at fourteen, at twenty one, at forty.
Boys will always be boys, even when they're men.

Everything is disappointing and it all seems
like the end of the world when no one hears
you and no one understands
and you try to put it on paper or on the internet
and people laugh and laugh and they just don't
take you seriously, but those tears you cry
behind a laptop or with your headphones on
in your bedroom all alone, in a house full of people,
blaring some emo band that's popular at the moment
is speaking to you better than any counselor
or therapist ever could.
Those tears they're real and they mean something
and you just think that you could die
right now and no one would care.

You're wrong, Brittany.
There's a Facebook memorial in your name.
There's a website coming soon.
You thought you were just some girl from New York
that people would forget about and I don't even know you
so why do I get sad when I see your picture and read
the words to a song that your father sang to you
where he called you "My Little Brit-ta-ny"?

Forty years, Brittany,
and my knives are down.
The hurt never leaves,
but I know you were wrong.

Firework

You are a brown ponytailed flash of
light, a burst of blue waves in
your eyes at seven am when we
both are exhausted from this
grind of public service.
I keep you near, like a little
sister and guard you from the
circling prey that would swallow
you. And when they try to separate
us, a long embrace shields us.

Middle poor

The author of a book about four suicides that happened in my town
summed up everyone's childhood there in two words:
middle poor.

My father, the garage doorman.
My mother, the reluctant housewife who
occasionally served us Swanson's Fried Chicken Dinners,
whose strangely seasoned corn would some how find its way
into the brownie in the middle of the aluminum tin.
It is a scent that I actually have nostalgia for.

As a middle poor child, I had a Big Wheel and
bikes my father would find put out for the trash
in the front of other yards that he would refurbish
with different shades of Krylon paint.

I think about how rich I felt wearing Lee jeans
and hideous striped shirts my mother bought at Sears,
as I count the change in my pocket and realize it is
all the money I have that isn't going towards bills.

Middle poor to poor poor in a small town filled
with people cashing their unemployment checks,
while I come home from work and peel off clothes
that smell like burnt bread, onions and vinegar
and earned me enough to maintain my internet,
my cable and just enough to pay my car on time.

This milk white, freckled, half Italian that shares
absolutely nothing with the likes of Snooki and J-Wow,
not even the right area code.

This creator of lines, this maker of sandwiches.

The Only Sister

She escaped as liquid
fleeing a flawed world,
leaving as a perfect ghost.
Maybe she saw me as a threat
and decided there was no room
for her in a house with a boy
and his Matchbox cars and a Big Wheel.
There would be no Barbie dolls to remove
the heads off of, no bullies to shove off
of her pink tricycle while she whined and sobbed
with grass stained knees on our front lawn by the
tiny Japanese maple tree that wouldn't survive, either.
A small plastic cube holds a white space among my baby pictures
where a faded picture of she and I would be, hugging for my father's
Kodak 110 camera, the only sister, the one I find in late night dreams.

Observations and reflections on a father

There are two hundred and forty days until
you officially become an octogenarian,
and the window on your diminished capacity is closing.
A simple job becomes a days-long project.
A trip to the grocery store for a few small
items becomes a debacle, with pantry shelves
resembling a fallout shelter's worth of supplies.
You cannot be trusted to watch your grandchildren alone.
Many of your days are now spent in various chairs around
the house, as you click and click through channels
and watch fifteen minutes of a movie that's already been on
for an hour before passing out with your head leaning.
I wonder if I will suffer the same fate, or if my
failing body will quit long before my mind does.

Tear in my side, I feel it all...

A wreck cannot take everything

When they pulled her from the wreckage,
her body as battered and crushed as the
vehicle, one of her limbs was swallowed
by the scene of the accident and left behind.

When she woke in the hospital bed, she
cried, asked me how she would be able to write
her name on an anniversary card without her
right hand, how I could love three quarters of a girl.

When doctors said they could not save the mangled
meat that remained of her left arm, she asked me
how she would be able to touch my face, to brush her
teeth, to hold a daughter, or me.

When her bruised, weary legs carried her through
our front door, I became her limbs, became her hands.
I skywrote forever hearts. She told me I loved half
a girl. I told her that we are a circle, a constant
and neverending love.

At night, I wrap her with my warmth, press my cheek to
hers, whisper in her ear, "You are stuck with 100% of me."

We are bound by sickness

You sit and watch internet videos of girls
with body dysmorphia disorder like you're
flipping through a catalog.

You bookmark anorexia sites
as if you are seeking tips
on how to follow through in secret.

I don't yet know if it is some sort
of weird fascination or if you plan
to carry out these things on your body
one day, your arms becoming a canvas
of onion skin, your face gaunt and colorless.

You don't know that I'm infatuated with
the hows and whys of my own demise.
I wonder if you'll study my drained body,
leave the bones behind while you consume
the death inside me.

Harbor

Those days when you walked meekly with
a tawny pony tail and a baseball hat,
kicking dirt and concealing your pain
in hide-and-seek games where you never
wished to be found, seem a distant reality
now that you have surfaced across my screen,
across miles and miles of terrain that
keep our fingers from touching, that
keep me from lifting you off your feet
in a long embrace. The years between us
are worn into our faces, both of us are
blonde now. I wait here for you to
uncloak me from the fog of your absence as
you announce your brazen, nomadic ways
to the world, make literal red marker
lines across the country and stick
temporary pins in cities, smuggle your
unrelenting warmth to the coldest regions.

Absent daughter

A box downstairs holds
a framed picture, a sun and
moon with eyes closed, the
words "sleep precious baby, sleep",
it was to hang in your room.

Dissolver

This winter sun scorches my retinas
like the eighty days of summer in Barrow -
it never seems to relent. You look up
anyway, the dark red in your brown hair
flashing like party lights in the blustery
air. You get impulsive, dart off into the
deep comforter of snow, leaving indents
in your wake, run staccato, diagonal, fall
awkwardly with a squeal. I am busy following
my own breath back to the idling car, only
hear a faint echo while you pull yourself up
and hobble back. I am always willing to hide
from anything that shines too brightly. Later,
in the walls between shared space, you show
me what sixty seven days of darkness is like.

Sea Blind

"We are all casualties of war," she says,
her voice on repeat in my skull as she
shows me the pink circle on her forearm,
the lump of bone bulging in her shin.
"Our vessels are laid to waste from the
first day we're alive," she tells me. I
picture lifeless lines of bodies, grasses
stained with blood. The fingers on her
hammer headed man hands bloat at the tips
and her eyes are always speckled her around
their brown centers. She's carrying the
weight of a broken engagement, bags of work
clothes and medicinal weed. She will
cauterize the wounds once again, while she
sips a glass of wine, while the dead haunt
her in black and white, while she dreams of
beaches not stained in red.

No apologies

The little presents you gave
the magic eight ball,
the framed movie poster of
Pulp Fiction, all have found
their way to a pile of
decomposing trash.

The cd's I pretended to like -
the ones you made for me,
will never spin and spin in
the mini stereo on my book shelf
ever again.

I've donated every shirt you've
given me to Goodwill.

I've purposely over-fed your fish.

I used your toothbrush to clean the
hair dye stains out of the tub.

I had your mail forwarded to a
random address I found in the phone book.

A few things bullying has taught me

I learned that I could run just a little faster
than George Beucler most of the time,
though sometimes he caught up and would bash me
over the head with his metal lunchbox.

I learned that some sixth grader despised me
so much that he would chase and torment me,
no matter what path I took home from school,
so I became more aware of my surroundings.

I learned that being an introvert wasn't such a
terrible thing when most of my afternoons were
spent listening to music and playing with toys
that I never had to share with anyone else.

I learned that the girls that tortured me the most,
the ones who glued my notebook shut, stuck gum
on my arm and joked about me in front of their friends
were the ones who actually liked me the most.

I learned that broken bones heal and
words become an outlet to quell the urges to give up,
even when they can be the very thing that tighten the noose.

Blister

A backhand to the
psyche, the snap and
retreat. The quiet is
comfort, is where
you gather all of your
words in defense,
then delete them all.
The bump grows, fills
with bile, with blood.
You keep it close, like
the memory of feet
traipsing across floors,
the shards too thick to
make it down the drain
that gather as a pained
memoria.

Stealing Babies
(for Jessica Whelan)

Near the end, it wouldn't let anything stay
in your stomach—food, medicine, even water.
It stole a little more of you each day,
left you with an unending anxiety, the pain
from a single hug. You were bound to a bed,
a needle in your thigh. Sleep was the only
escape from constant agony. Black and white
photos captured each phase of your darkness,
of an enemy who fed on you from within. Your
nerves played cruel games with you, all
screaming at the same time, finding their
voice through your cries. Control had been
lost, in every facet, leaving you a mine,
excavated of its usefulness. Sleep was mercy,
was the final embrace after your father's
kisses. This thief fled after your final
exhale. This gatherer of youth, this brutal
blood menace.

Meet me at the back of the crowd, this could be our time to slip away...

Adalynn decides it's time to go

You were supposed to make a full recovery.
No one ever expected this.
Now you get to be two and a half forever.

You never had the chance to try peanut butter
on bread, in chocolate, on your fingers as you
unscrew the top of the jar while your parents
are asleep in their beds, the tasty spread
stuck under your little fingernails.

Never had the opportunity to experience the
exhilaration of riding a tricycle, your feet
pedaling quickly, the wind whipping around
your pink helmet and blowing the tassels on
your handlebars, making them look like streamers
in the hot Texas summer air.

All that remains are numbers.
288 days in a hospital.
28 surgeries, several infections.
3 times, your heart stopped.
On the last one, you'd had enough.

My female friends are mostly brunettes

who write poems when they're not doing readings
in the midwest or visiting museums or fighting
off type 2 diabetes or fighting themselves
in a barely lit living room with a glass
of wine. They are dyeing their hair, joining
Ok Cupid, flossing in their bra and panties
in the kitchen. They are posting cute statuses
on Facebook, sending drunken tweets on Twitter,
getting high on Tumblr. They are moving into
big ass houses in the country, they are making
little books in big cities, they are flaunting
their curves in cursive.

In case there's any confusion

Not all boys rape, Rehteah.
There are boys that know better
than to ply a girl with so much
alcohol that she can't possibly
make a rational decision or
consent to have sex with one boy,
let alone four of them.

Not all boys think it's funny
to send pictures of the gang rape
over their smartphones to their
friends and post them online.

Not every single boy in Canada,
in the US, in the civilized world
is going to call a girl a slut
for being someone's vessel that
is left to piece together the events
the next morning, the next week, month.

You found your answer in a rope
and I'm tired of writing poems to
dead girls who hang themselves,
dead girls who think that these stupid
boys deserve to hold that much power
over them, dead girls who gets cheated
out of the bliss of incredible music,
the sight of New York City's skyline,
the amazing waves of California's coast.

It wasn't fucking worth it, Rehteah.
Never let little bastards like that win.

Losing Cheyenne

On the chalkboard wall in my office
you wrote your name along the corner
near the door frame, drew a pink heart
and some strange design closer to the
floor, wrote the words "Hi, I love you
guys." I'll keep the memories of you
belting out a Drowning Pool song with
your own lyrics - "Let the bodies hit
the beach!", riding go-karts in Ocean
City. All you want to do now is get high.

The perfect way to drown

My father is the reason I never learned
to swim. I would sit by the edge of our
neighbor's pool and dangle my feet over
the side just enough to cover them, just
enough to be able to stare all the way
down to the blue liner at the bottom as
the chlorinated water rippled. I'd watch
the plastic vent door open and shut,
open and shut, duck away when someone
threw a beach ball near me, my thick red
hair in my eyes. Getting my feet wet wasn't
enough for my father. He'd always think it
was hilarious to push me into the water.
My body would sink like a pale anchor,
the water stinging my sinuses, my stunned
mouth agape and swallowing. My head crested
the water in what seemed like slow motion
and my clogged ears could still hear my
father laughing, as if this was the shove
that would make me want to take swimming
lessons. Instead, it gave me an out, a way
to rid myself of the voices in my head.
Knives are painful and it takes too long
for them to finish the job. I could just
wait until my neighbors had gone off to open
their bakery and rattle their wood gate ajar.
Dressed in a long sleeve shirt and cords,
my feet weighted with combat boots, I'll pull
the cover off of the pool and slip slowly over
the side, feel myself become weightless, watch
my arms flail up, like they're waving goodbye
and feel the water dragging me to the bottom.

Dementia Valediction

It has been a slow build
to the end, these last
few years. I eat two
breakfasts sometimes.
I tell stories about
your mom and her friend
punching me while I'm
in my bed. It seems so
real, it must be. I'm
not sure. Sometimes,
I know there's something
wrong in my head. All
I do is eat and sleep.
I think about ending it
myself, but I'm not sure
how I'd go about that.
When I leave the house,
I drive the same streets
over and over. Sometimes,
I see my work on garages
in different neighborhoods.
I think about not coming
back home. It doesn't
matter much when you can't
remember the names of your
grandchildren. I think I
remember you. Your voice
is familiar, so I'll say
my goodbyes now while I
can still know why I'm
doing it.

Valediction for an ex-girlfriend

My mother called on a Sunday,
told me you were gone.
She didn't know much more.
I knew what you told me on Facebook.
The bad marriage and divorce,
the older guy who got you hooked
on drugs, the bulimia,
the pictures you posted online,
gaunt, bony and frail.
It wasn't the same girl I dated,
but you were smiling. Somehow,
after everything your 35 year old
body endured, you managed to smile.
You had a husband who treated you well,
you'd just gotten a new cat.
You also kept throwing up.
It had to be what finally beat you,
the last strain on a fragile ecosystem.
I want you to know that I let go of
that bitterness some years ago,
that I had a fight with my wife over
being in contact with you again.
After I hung up the phone with my mother,
I asked my wife if I should feel sad.
I think I finally do, Jessica.

Katie, disappearing

I thought it was water or coffee
thrown at me by some crazy, scruffy
homeless guy. I thought I'd have to
go home and change my clothes over
someone's rudeness until I felt the
pain sink in, until I could feel skin
coming off and watched my clothes
disappear, saw my flesh turning red,
bubble and dissolve. Everything looked
cloudy. I could hear screams and didn't
even know they were mine, my voice, a
gravelly, acid coated stranger. Pieces
of me were disappearing and I couldn't do
a thing to stop it. I felt like my bones
were on fire, like the end was near
and I was this pitiful sight, gawked at
by people. No one would help me. I knew
it was Danny's idea, knew that only he
could inflict this kind of misery, knew
that raping me two days before wasn't
enough. He had to erase me.

I am everything I've ever eaten

I am every slice of pizza from every
pizza shop I have ever set foot in.
I am boxes of Cheez-Its and more cups
of coffee than I'll ever be able to count.
I am Snapple Peach Iced Tea. I don't drink
it anymore, but it's there, lingering in
the back of my eyes, left a dark mark on
my right toe. I am bacon. Holy fuck, I am
bacon times infinity. I am malted milk balls
and Tootsie Rolls. I am lots of soft serve,
especially in my midsection. I am well
preserved, so fuck you, cancer. I've already
beaten you down once. I am Lotrel, swimming
down my throat, controlling the flow of blood.
I am salad from Panera, from Saladworks, from
Wawa, from my kitchen, helping me to keep a
healthy sheen. I am air. I am a bullet.

In vitro
for N

Hello spark.
Your charge starts this flame
inside of me. Right now,
it is a slow, blue light
like a bunsen burner.
You are a jigsaw piece,
an unbroken yolk I can't see
but can keep warm.
You should know how we labored
for you, even when my cells
were found faulty, even when
the broken pieces were gutted
from my womb.
Now it is about making phone calls
with cautious excitement,
about growing you from the
ground up, thick roots spread
from Poland to America,
to you in a petri dish.
I stand in front of the mirror,
place my pale hands over flatlands
that you will expand,
release a long breath and begin
my wait for you.

Tourniquet

Your memory is a pantry cleaned
of food, a shelf of peeled up
paper and two ants fighting for
the last stale crumb.

Your love was a tourniquet.

Your scent is fried chicken,
a hated summer job. You peeled
those work wears and picked lily
of the valley, lit candles, cooked
me food I'd never eaten -
scallops, imitation crab.

You wrote poems, I threw them away.

Your breath, a wisp in the humid
air. What is left of you scattered,
mingling with earth, a notion.
I probably never loved you.

You need the darkness if you want to see stars

An echo through the humid air. An ache deep
in shins keeps you grounded, keeps you hidden
from the passing cars and the sound of the
mailman delivering bills and death notices.
At night, between the raindrops and floating
pieces of tree sheddings, you crane your head
up into the night's thickness, look for intervention,
seek a solace only solitude can provide. Over and
over, you cut at scars, hide out in your trenches.
Erase the pieces you despise, one by one.

They try to fix you but sorrow's in the marrow...

The Punisher

There are a few days during the month
that I don't feel like I have to vomit,
where I can sit in silence and stare
out the darkened windows and listen to
the rain and wind batter the crumbling
shingles on the roof and pretend that
every drop is a release from my own
body, that refuses to shed a single tear.

Most days, my body is a battering ram,
is a ramshackle shed in the middle of a
forest, where water pools in the corners
and squirrels bury their food for the
winter. Most days, I am car crash, am
the tree fed into the wood chipper. Most
days, my reflection is the only truth,
the razor blade shaking in wet hands,
a looped recording that says *Fuck you*,
that says, *You are shit*, that says,
Just give up.

Tonight, I am that squirrel, run down in
the middle of the street, insides spilled
on asphalt. Tonight, blood can wash away
in the downpour. Tonight, I can again hide,
inside the unfinished novel sitting on my
desk, the half written short stories where
everyone dies, in the bathroom, the only
place I can weep in peace, where truth is
a full length mirror, a room with towels
to muffle the sound.

The night we tried to run away

I didn't make it back in time to
pick you up from work. You gave
in to your nerves, hid in a fort
made of blankets. I made the mistake
of texting you the words "I love you."
You enrolled in culinary classes at
the local college. I spent the night
convincing myself that you would ditch
me for a late night Walmart run. You
couldn't bear to share the space between
your arms with me.

For the girl with the Golden State in her eyes

This is a knock on the wood
door that keeps you sheltered
from the people that throw away
your kindness. This is the text
message that wipes away doubt.
This is the email to keep you
from spending the night alone
on your bed, as you rock yourself
and cry, wanting to die. This is
the note in the sky saying, "Don't
give up.", the Facebook post
saying, "He's not fucking worth
it." This is me, telling you,
that everything is not bullshit,
that an embrace is more powerful
than a razor.

On masturbating over people you may never meet
(after Trista Mateer)

You occupy little space in their scripts.
The tissue box is nearby—it is the consolation
after the crying. You do it alone, as the sun
blasts through thin curtains. You think that
the mail carrier can't see you, can't feel the
desperation, the arms so tired of being open
that one droops to the side while the other is
frantic. No one can hear you gasp, no one will
hold you when it's over. You spend under five
minutes calling to a god you don't even believe
in. You throw your head back and release, listen
for a sigh, a crack of the hip, a whispered "Oh,
baby"—hope you're a phone's buzz, a notification,
a slow slide of a finger across a screen.

If you're gonna go, go big

I save what I discard in bottles
and hide them in my dresser,
in my closet and under the bed.
I can feel the cells leaving me
every day. I am becoming translucent,
transcendent. I don't need the
mirror anymore. I have never felt
better about myself than now,
as I watch purple circles form
around my eyes. I don't even need
clothes anymore. I pass through
air and space so light of foot,
so full of grace. This is my last
ballet and I will arabesque to my
last breath, smiling as I pass.

Tell it to the kids

in Philly. The teenaged fuckers who
attacked two Temple students with
bricks. Those five girls who left
another girl, someone they did not
know, with broken teeth. Tell them
that bricks give you no power. Bricks
build the homes they live in for free.
Bricks make foundations. They also can
take away your IPhones, your freedom.
Tell them that words are more powerful.
Tell them that a girl with no teeth
can still speak well enough to put you
in jail. Tell them that compassion is
a more powerful weapon against boredom.

The monster of Riverside

He writes you letters now, begging
for understanding. It is easy to
repent when he is locked away, unable
to dig into the underworld of underage
girls - laid out like eye candy for
sick minds. You are conflicted. He has
left you swollen, to care for another
mouth. He has been alone with your
daughter. His name, in newspapers and
on the internet. There is no erasing
the sight of handcuffs, the hundreds
of files on his laptop of little girls,
the picture of him standing behind you
in a Scream mask, his hands in the air
behind you while you hold your child.
Images burning your skin, holding you
captive.

For the girl who ran away

The book and two movies you lent me are
sitting on the bookshelf in my office.
I'm not done with them yet, though
you might be done with me. It has been
nearly three weeks since I saw your
face, thirteen days since you posted
a writing prompt on your blog. You
became a weekend migraine's victim,
a flowered dress on Easter. You are
a phantom behind a screen, a poet with
no words to offer. The curtains are
gathering dust. Soon, they will crumble.

You were the wrong exit

I wore you like a bruise,
weirdly shaped and purpled
on the back of my hand.
There is no pleasure in that
kind of pain. The slightest
graze and I wince. Your face
is a map to a dead end road.
In a matter of days, you turned
yellow, remained only a nuisance,
a faded book page, unable to inflict.

I am trying so very badly to be good

but most of the time, I am just thinking
of the shortest path to the end. I think
knives - car crash - pills, lots of pills.
I think of being bloated, throwing up,
exploding hearts and melted livers like
a stick of butter left in a microwave.
I try to distract myself with so much
coffee that my bladder bulges. The ache
in my neck comes back, a pain runs down my
arm. People want you to stay to forget
about how much they hate themselves.
I hate myself more. We are all selfish.
We all search for the last breath's relief.

I am breaking my bones to fit into places

I desperately need to be, like the curve
of your legs, the arch of your foot. Like
the Golden Gate Bridge, the coastline of
Nova Scotia, the sleeves of your jacket.
I push my achy joints to their breaking
point to touch the things you've left
behind, like your headphones, the cord
balled up in knots, like the dog, who is
confused and missing you. I listen closely
for the snap. It is when I love you the most.
It is the only gift I can give you now that
you've put on your boots and took that swan
dive. I want to be that brave. I want us
to fuck boneless. I want redemption.

What We Have (To Change)

The collection of old receipts on the dining
room table—they need to get tossed. The three
way light bulb that flickers in the lamp on
your side of the sofa. The gutter that removes
itself from the side of the house when it's
too windy. The way we don't speak about dying,
and how I don't want a funeral. The front door
that we have to slam closed, and the dead bolts,
and the peeling paint on the steps. The way I
feel ugly when you fall asleep before me every
night.

Hiding out in trenches I've built, I'm so good at it now, I know how to trick myself...

Are you dazzled by the same constellation?

The one that shines brighter than any
night sky that draped over our old,
outdated house? You raise a finger
and play connect the dots with the
stars, each shining like holes in the
black paper of a Lite Brite. We look
for Venus, wonder if other galaxies can
see into our front yard, if they stare
at the overgrown evergreens and judge
us. I slip my goosebumped arm around
your back, your head still craned to
the sky. You are caught in some other
orbit.

Always hollow, chasing shadows

that move in different shapes across barren
landscapes of empty. You think salvation
is the embrace you lack, spill words like wine
over concrete. The shadows move on, consume
another empty shell. You are a leafless tree
left browned, never to bloom in another's
orbit. You are lips chapped and pained. The
stiff breeze at your back, a harsh farewell,
a push to silence, to anyone who can wash
the ground in front of you with renewal.

My fingers were matches

that would ignite when I ran them
in circles along your hips. Now,
they barely spark, are left only
with a flash and the smell of
sulphur. We leave on bathroom
lights to find a path, rely on
instinct, stay perfectly still.
Your body is an eroded cliff, a
steep drop off away from plunging
into shallow water where necks
crack and nothing survives.

Sinister

Sometimes, a monster is a husband,
is a criminal, someone you keep
taking back, even after he has been
sent to prison. This monster bound you
with electrical cords and duct taped
your mouth, your silence, a certainty.
Warning signs be damned - love matters
more than his addictions, than bruises.
You had to make this work. Little girls
need fathers. You were found in repose,
a stilled life mother, sister, daughter.
How long did you lie under the brush
and branches, held by the brutal winter
in nothing more than a blanket?

Thief
(for Steve)

Your ex wants to move to Arizona to start
a new life, to roll with the punches
for a while. You will uproot yourself
to stay with your boy—his innocence
still intact. Right now, he fumbles
with a large cup for his hot chocolate,
changes his mind and gets an ICEE instead.
He wears a scar on his face, you carry
yours like a locked, steel box in your
chest—speaking in code in front of him,
mentally censoring your frustration.
Your wrists are weakened, cannot handle
the weight of tools, the turning of door
knobs. Still, you tell me to fight the
voice in my head that tells me to quit.
Still, you will wake in the morning after
losing a friend to suicide, and make your
corny jokes, take my abuse over another
Eagles loss. Each piece quietly stolen
from your grasp becomes fodder, becomes
focus. She cannot steal a forged bond.

Dusty Trails

You watch snow race down through
the front windows, and scatter over
the windshields of parked cars,
the already coated roofs of nearby
houses, tell me that you have had
enough of this cold, that you'll run
away to somewhere warm with me. I say
California, without hesitation, and
add Venice Beach, like I've mapped an
escape route from this state where I've
watched too many people vanish. Soon,
I am flush with images: you curled
in the passenger seat of my thirteen
year old car—your darkened toes in the
pale west coast sand—your dark spirals
of hair draped over my shoulder as you
nap in the afternoon. This life is never
kind to anyone who drags complacent feet
over the same trails, but we are writers,
good only at building lives that will never
be ours. Our hands join and squeeze, then
separate into an unforgiving March wind.

I'll climb any tower, take any grand notion

but I'll just settle for the follow through,
for you to show up at one of my readings one
day, for you to not flinch when I touch your
arm, for the trepidation of intimacy to wash
away under my embrace. I'll settle for the
feel of your thick turtleneck sweater against
my face, for your voice to raise above a low
rumble, for the spaces between my fingers to
be where yours would slip into like deliverance,
like how our bodies curl like commas in the
perfect sentence, the story where we begin.

Feels So Different

In the wake of a faux pas,
when sharing space in a
room, on a sofa, in a bed,
feels like playtime, feels
like a plodding book you
keep reading in hopes of a
turnaround, a revelation.
A face can seem less trusting,
can look like an imposter,
the outline of a vow that has been
crossed out with black marker.
It feels the neighbor's
doberman, who knows you, who
sees you every day, but could
easily take a chunk from your
hand as you pet him. It feels
like the past on repeat. It
feels like another ending.

For the girl who wants to save the planet

You ask for an address to send
me an actual letter, a decorated
envelope with a long letter and
pictures of your latest trip,
your hand extended to mine from
wherever you are resting your head
tonight. You are a closed cropped,
dark haired explosion over the
backdrop of a lake. You are bound
to nothing, and no single person.
Know this: your kindness has pulled
me from a dark place. Know this:
your words describe a version of me
I do not recognize, but hope that
you keep tucked away in your pocket.
Know this: you can find me among the
clutter of newsfeeds and bickering,
in the silence of the late evening,
to rest your burdened head on my
shoulder to cry, judgment left on a
dusty shelf to fester alone.

You are not a national holiday

The trash will still be picked up.
The sky will cloud over, and fog
will roll in over the numb side
streets, keeping a thick hush.
No stores will be closing early.
I will dig into drawers and look
for the instruction manual, turn
towards the back, almost into the
French directions and find that
the fault was mine all along, even
when the words aren't clear. I will
find the last shred of dignity,
wasting away in the back of the coat
closet, push it deep into my pocket,
and carry it off with me, escape
the riddles and silence.

Mettle

(for JD)

There is no time to wallow.
There are jobs to be done—
in retail, where you spend
nights in a parking lot,
sit in a car with a walkie
talkie and plot playlists
for weekend parties, your
massive collection, an
endless loop that keeps
bodies moving, much like yours.
Tests bring relief that age
has not robbed you of anything
just yet, that you still go out
in the morning for two cups of
coffee, talk to me about music
and football, and make your wife
wonder if you had roasted the
beans yourself by the time you
finally get home. The threat of
failing organs never diminished
your vitality, never plundered
the luster you carry in your face.
Today, you were in absentia.

I hope I never have a daughter

so that she doesn't have to have her
long red hair pulled by some stupid
boy who will make fun of her and tell
her that she has no soul. I hope I
never have a daughter that looks
anything like me, that has star cluster
freckles over her shoulders and arms,
like me, that carries the weight of
melancholy like a pocket full of stones
that she has swiped from the edges of
curbs and along train tracks. I hope I
never have a daughter who scrapes used
razors over her wrists to feel something
other than emptiness and nausea in her
gut. I hope I never have a daughter who
wakes up behind a dumpster, on a strange
carpet with dried vomit on her face and
clothes, who doesn't know why she aches
everywhere, who gives too much of herself
until there is nothing left for her to do but
find every pill in the house and use them
to quiet all of the noise. I hope I never
have a daughter who has to carve pieces
of herself off in front of mirrors, who
slowly disappears as soon as she blends in.
I hope I never have a daughter—
this world doesn't fucking deserve her.

This world is only gonna break your heart

So I left you sitting at a table at some
truck stop diner off of a dusty interstate
in the middle of nowhere. The bill is paid,
the tip, still on the table. You won't find
my car in the parking lot, just the tire
marks left behind in the gravel and dirt.
There is nothing else I can give you besides
a full belly, an unwanted inconvenience.
Words will leave you as empty as that Coke
bottle rattling around the highway's edge.
I do this only to prove that I've never been
anyone's answer. I say these things to show
you that I am as broken as you, that you
cannot gather two shattered things from the
ground and make them one breathing thing,
something that won't end up as roadkill,
fed on by crows and flies.

Oh, Jupiter

You can swallow all of your neighbors
whole—suck them into your orbit and
bleed them dry of their nutrients,
grow like Ursula in the deep of the
ocean, holding Triton's scepter,
becoming more and more powerful. Your
permanent bruise shifting, spinning.
Who hurt you? Who left you a shell of
a giant? We all marvel at you on Earth,
watch you through curved glass, see
Hubble's pictures—stalking you like
interplanetary paparazzi. You never
wane. You stay docile, unfazed. Our
feet would freeze upon entry to your
massive mouth. We write odes to you,
you just spin and spin—introverted and
filled with scars and resignation.

A meditation via subtraction

In place of his mouth is a silencer,
a needle and black thread. (He is not
allowed to use the pink.) In place of
his mouth is closed sign, a for rent
sign. In place of his mouth are white
flags waving. In place of his mouth
are someone else's lips, speaking in
French, speaking in Russian. In place
of his mouth, is a list of things he
could have been if he listened to his
mother. In place of his mouth is a
canvas, a set of watercolors. In place
of his mouth is an eraser.

Monsters

You would put rat poison in the shopping cart
as you and your mother walked the aisles of
Kmart. It was a not so subtle hint that you
would rather spend the remaining years of
your youth caged among junior criminals
than spend another day under siege in what
is supposed to be the safest place: your own
home. You do not speak of the beatings, the
times he threatened to kill both of you, only
the relief of his death, the heart attack that
saved your life. You have pictures of the
three of you in the basement, buried in
yellowed binder sleeves, evidence of what
a monster could look like. You pass the
cemetery where his shell rests on your daily
drive to work, tell me that you have no idea
where he is buried. You no longer jump at
the slightest touch, fists bared. You sleep
above the covers now, exposed and tranquil.

Kendall A. Bell's poetry has been most recently published in Anti-Heroin Chic and Philosophical Idiot. He was nominated for Sundress Publications' Best of the Net collection in 2007, 2009, 2011, 2012, 2013 and 2015. He is the author of twenty four chapbooks. His current chapbook is called "Chasing The Skyline". He is the founder and co-editor of the online journal Chantarelle's Notebook and publisher/editor of Maverick Duck Press. His chapbooks are available through Maverick Duck Press. He lives in Southern New Jersey.

www.ingramcontent.com/pod-product-compliance
Lightning Source LLC
LaVergne TN
LVHW091227080426
835509LV00009B/1201

* 9 7 8 0 6 9 2 1 6 7 8 3 0 *